Let it Rain

Peace in the Perfect Will of God

Dr Desryn T. A. Collins

WESTBOW
PRESS®
A DIVISION OF THOMAS NELSON
& ZONDERVAN

This book is a work of non-fiction. Unless otherwise noted, the author
and the publisher make no explicit guarantees as to the accuracy of
the information contained in this book and in some cases, names of
people and places have been altered to protect their privacy.

WestBow Press books may be ordered through booksellers or by contacting:

WestBow Press
A Division of Thomas Nelson & Zondervan
1663 Liberty Drive
Bloomington, IN 47403
www.westbowpress.com
844-714-3454

Scripture quotations are taken from the New King James Version. Copyright
© 1982 by Thomas Nelson, Inc. Used by permission. All rights reserved.

ISBN: 979-8-3850-2576-3 (sc)
ISBN: 979-8-3850-2577-0 (e)

Library of Congress Control Number: 2024910228

Print information available on the last page.

WestBow Press rev. date: 06/25/2024

Contents

Introduction

This book was written with you in mind. Yes, *you* – the Christian who earnestly desires to walk with God. It was also written for me. God expects us to walk boldly and live abundantly as His children. He wants us to come up higher and he is pointing us to the way to do just that. These are challenging times for Christians, but they are also exciting times if we live as if we truly believe God's word.

This precious book is a compilation of inspirational thoughts on some of the most crucial issues that confront us from day to day. Each entry is a complete and independent message rooted on the principles of the Bible. Each one was written with total reliance on the Holy Spirit to shed light on our way as we journey to the Promised Land. Most of the messages were originally shared as blog posts on my blog, *Crystal Treasures*, and I firmly believe that in every one of them God was speaking directly to me and ministering to my needs. I know they will minister to you too.

It would be great if you started at the beginning and read right on to the last entry but that is not necessary. You can jump into the messages at any entry that piques your interest or speaks to your current need. Just read prayerfully and let the Holy Spirit open your mind and help you to understand the truths that God wants you to accept.

After you have read this book, your life will be transformed. You will continue your walk with God with new ways of interpreting all of your experiences. You will discover joyful truths and inscriptions of hope in everyday occurrences. God's Word, the Holy Scriptures will come alive in remarkable ways, inspiring you to walk boldly with your God. Most of all, as you witness the events that are unfolding around the world, you will enjoy perfect peace.

I am a fellow traveler,

Desryn T. A. Collins

1

Truth, Most Certain

If you are a Christian walking with God, celebrate the momentous events that are unfolding around the world. Currently, life on Earth is characterised by shocking killings, economic turmoil, social decadence, medical morass and perverse weather patterns. Generally, projections for the future of the planet are dismal. There seems to be very little to celebrate because, evidently, the world is spiralling towards a catastrophic end. And it is, but it is this very fact that is worth celebrating. You see, the end of the world as we know it, is not the end if you're walking with God, and that is **the absolute truth**.

It does not matter which region of the world you live because no part of the globe is free from current or impending turmoil. The whole world is engulfed in a cyclone of trouble and life will become significantly more treacherous. There will be greater economic turmoil, sea levels will continue to rise, and many more catastrophic natural disasters will occur around the globe. Nations will rise against nations, and there will be increased unrests and displacements. That is the dismal truth. Yet, when we witness these occurrences, we should not despair. Rather, it is time to celebrate. We do not celebrate what is presently happening in our world; we celebrate what will happen thereafter.

The Certainty of God's Word

Let us focus on the whole story. The headlines reveal what's happening, but without the context of the great controversy between good and evil. If we ignore the assurance of the promises of God, we could get preoccupied with current events and overlook what those events signify. As Christians, it is extremely important that we consistently view current events as the magnificent unfolding of truth. The Word of God, the Holy Bible, not only tells us about the times in which we live, but it tells us that these dismal times signal that something glorious is about to happen. Yes, you read that right, something glorious is about to happen. So, don't be distressed by the headlines; marvel at the certainty of God's word.

Perilous Times

The only reliable index of the future is the word of God in which we are told, "But know this, that in the last days perilous times will come" (2 Timothy 3:1, NKJV) Paul, the apostle who penned this letter to Timothy, was merely reiterating what Jesus

Himself outlined in Matthew Chapter 24. Jesus painted a very vivid picture of what the world would be like in the last days of Earth's history. Wars, rumours of wars, nations rising against nations, famines, diseases, natural disasters, the proliferation of imposters claiming to be prophets, were all foretold. I know how horrifying the stories we hear and read about are. I know that there are days when your faith is shaken by what is reported or what you experience. Indeed, these are perilous times.

Hope amidst the Perils

These perilous times mean we are in the last days. Jesus came to Earth to restore man to His Creator. Sin separated man from God but Jesus died for the sins of mankind and He returned to heaven promising that He will return for those who believe in Him. In John 14: 1-3 we read, "Let not your heart be troubled; you believe in God, believe also in Me. In My Father's house are many mansions; if it were not so, I would have told you. I go to prepare a place for you. And if I go and prepare a place for you, I will come again and receive you to Myself; that where I am, there you may be also." (NKJV) This promise, juxtaposed with Jesus' description of the events of the last days should engender hope, not fear, peace, not despair.

Even in these perilous times, God is ever close to the believer. Declarations of His love surround us. Jesus said, "I have come that they may have life, and that they may have it more abundantly." (John 10:10 NKJV) Abundant living comes through the mindset with which we approach life. Life on earth will never be perfect, but we can have perfect peace if we learn to trust God implicitly and to read the love messages He sends us regularly.

God's Messages of Love

There isn't a day that goes by that God doesn't remind us of His love. The glowing sun, a baby's smile, the laughter of friends, the joy of giving, the gentle breeze and twinkling stars, a life guard's wave, a bird's sweet song, medical miracles and musical notes, a generous heart and seeing eyes, honest deeds and growing trees all provide us with undeniable assurances that we can hold fast to the belief that God loves us with an everlasting love. God reminds us in all of our life experiences, both good and bad, and in the acts of nature, pleasant and unpleasant, that He loves us and cares about our eternal destiny. It is because of His love for us that He sent His Son to die so we can be saved. John 3:16 says, "For God so loved the world that He gave His only begotten Son, that whosoever believes in Him should not perish but have everlasting life" (NKJV). God wants us to experience eternal life. He knows that we are living in perilous times.

So, it is true that the headlines are dismal and discouraging, but the story doesn't end there. All the terrible things happening in the world signal the imminent destruction of sin and the world that currently exists. The world is coming to an end AND something glorious is about to happen. Jesus is coming again! Jesus is coming again! Jesus told His disciples that when all the things that are currently happening are taking place, it means that "it [His coming] is near – at the doors!" Matthew 24:33.

What does Jesus's coming mean for you and me? The Bible says, "And God will wipe away every tear from their eyes; there shall be no more death, nor sorrow, nor crying. There shall be no more pain, for the former things have passed away." (Revelation 21:4, NKJV)

What a glorious promise! Yes, the headlines are distressing, but don't dwell on the headlines; focus on the certainty of God's word, and the blessed hope it provides. Keep trusting God. Hold on to his promises because His word assures us that "he who endures to the end shall be saved." (Matthew 24:13, NKJV).

While you take note of the terrifying headlines, remember, that's not the end of the story. If you believe that Jesus loves you and that He died to save you, there is hope for you. Soon, He will come again and all tears will be wiped away. There shall be no more death. That is the certain truth.

2

Keep Walking

Those who will inherit eternal life must **walk** with God. It is not the physical act of walking that is referred to here; it is the spiritual journey we take as children of God. Walking is a metaphor for the Christian life and I believe God was intentional in choosing the verb 'walk' to represent this spiritual journey. When Moses instructed God's people in Deuteronomy 5: 33 to "Walk in all the ways the Lord your God has commanded you, that you may live and that it may be well with you" (NKJV), he was declaring what God expects of all His followers for all times.

Walking, I am told, is an excellent form of exercise and exercise, we all know, is essential for good health. People who walk regularly make an investment in their physical and mental condition. In addition to burning calories and reducing weight, walking prevents atrophy of muscles and other essential tissues, safeguards the functions of the heart, the liver and the kidneys and it keeps the body in shape. It is definitely my preferred form of exercise.

Walking requires effort and it does not happen in one spot. You have to take steps for your action to be considered walking. It is a dynamic activity. When I am walking, three things are bound to change: my pace, my location and my condition.

I can take a brisk walk or a leisurely stroll, move confidently with even steps or stumble along with uncertainty. When I take a walk, the path that I choose may be dangerous or it may pose no threat at all. A smooth road could be followed by a rough stretch, the way may change from an upward climb to a pelt down a hill. Nothing is constant when I am walking. Change in location is inevitable and so is change in my condition.

My emotional and mental conditions change depending on what I encounter on the walk and my emotional state at the start of my journey. On a long walk, a gloomy mood gives way to joy but the opposite is also possible. I may set off on my walk feeling happy and optimistic but witness a harrowing act of injustice or experience some difficulty which makes me feel depressed. Generally, though, walking improves my mood. While I am out walking, I can also learn a lot about the environment. The stimulation of the senses - sight, hearing, smell, taste and touch - that a walk permits is guaranteed to promote learning so intellectual growth also occurs.

Notable changes also happen to my physical condition during the course of a walk. My muscles stretch and feelings of fatigue give way to new bursts of energy. I don't just break a sweat, my body is toned and tensions are released from my limbs. I have found out that walking is multifaceted in its benefits and significance.

It is no coincidence that walking is used as a metaphor for life and, particularly, the Christian journey. While we wait for the second coming of Jesus and an end to the turmoil in the world, we would do well to remind ourselves regularly to keep walking.

Walking before God

When God instructed Abraham in Genesis 17 to walk before Him (I am Almighty God; walk before Me and be blameless. Verse 1 NKJV), His choice of verb was deliberate. God wanted Abram to make a connection between all that walking signifies and his faith life. Most importantly, He was letting Abram know that he would never be alone. Life was a journey and He, Almighty God, was always going to be with Abram. We, too, should embrace this metaphor and all it signifies. Let's examine the analogy between walking and the Christian life a little more closely.

Change is Inevitable

God's instruction to Abram to 'walk' before him was a way of informing Abram that there were no constants other than His presence on Abram's journey through life. God wanted Abram to understand that his pace would change, his location would shift and his condition would be transformed. The metaphor of walking suggests that sometimes he would move briskly and make great progress but sometimes he might stumble, stall, or stop to refresh himself. There are times when he would find himself on the wrong path and have to change course. Sometimes, he would be exuberant but sometimes he would be dejected. God's instruction to Abram is His instruction to each of us who professes to be a Christian. It is His instruction to me. It is what He expects of you. "Walk before me" is what He says.

Keeping in Form

In order to be in perfect form for the Christian walk, we have to stay close to God and love our fellowmen. We stay close to God by praying and studying God's word. When Jesus walked on Earth, he rose up early in the morning to pray. He gained strength from constant communion with His Father. Jesus is our ultimate example but the Bible is filled with accounts of victories that were wrought by the followers of God through prayer. Prayer is the power we need to energize us for our Christian walk. Do not neglect to pray.

2 Timothy 2:15 admonishes us to "Be diligent to present yourself approved to God, a worker who does not need to be ashamed, rightly dividing the word of truth" (NKJV). Bible study is an essential practice for Christians. There is no circumstance that you can face in life that the word of God does not have instructions for. In God's word, you can find all the answers you need for every situation you are likely to face. Your preparation must precede your encounter with the wiles of the devil. There is no question about whether or not you will face the enemy of your soul. As long as you are on the Lord's side, Satan will hurl fiery darts of temptations and trials your way but if you are firmly grounded in the truth, you will be

able to meet his onslaughts the way Jesus did. Study God's word regularly and meaningfully so that you can meet every challenge with the words, "It is written".

Prayer and Bible study keep us connected to God and this connection informs how we relate to our fellowmen. The Christian walk has a vertical and a horizontal dimension. Just as we are careful to strengthen our relationship with God, we should be careful to strengthen our relationship with our fellowmen. 1 John 4:11 says, "Beloved, if God so loved us, we also ought to love one another" (NKJV). We cannot claim to love our fellowmen, if the way we relate to them is not consistent with the description of love that is found in 1 Corinthians 13. The principles of love that are outlined in God's word can only manifest in our lives when we surrender our will to God. By nature, we are selfish and unloving but through the power of the Holy Spirit, we can grow in our walk with God and shine a light in this dark world of sin. It's not easy but you have been called to walk before God.

Don't Give Up

Understand, clearly, that on your Christian journey, you can always count on God's presence. As much as you pray and study God's word, you are likely to experience periods of doubt. There are going to be times when the challenges are so great that you question the love of God and are tempted to give up. Don't. He is always watching over you. God sees your every move and He never stops taking care of you. Romans 8:35-39 says, "Who shall separate us from the love of Christ? Shall tribulation, or distress, or persecution, or famine, or nakedness, or peril, or sword? As it is written:

> "For Your sake we are killed all day long;
> We are accounted as sheep for the slaughter."

Yet in all these things we are more than conquerors through Him who loved us. For I am persuaded that neither death nor life, nor angels nor principalities nor powers, nor things present nor things to come, nor height nor depth, nor any other created thing, shall be able to separate us from the love of God which is in Christ Jesus our Lord." (NKJV)

God knows all of the challenges we are likely to encounter while we walk. He knows that we may get weary, but He has instructed us to keep moving. That's the essence of the metaphor. In Psalm 121: 7-8 we are told, "The Lord shall preserve you from all evil; He shall preserve your soul. The Lord shall preserve your going out and your coming in from this time forth, and even forevermore" (NKJV). Keep moving. Nobody walks in one spot.

So, my friend, yesterday might not have been such a great day but move on. You might have made some mistakes and misrepresented your faith. Just don't turn your back on God. If you want to be among those who will inherit eternal life, then keep walking with God. His promises are sure. He says in Deuteronomy 31:6 that he would never leave us, so walk in the power of his promise. Life may be steep but don't give up. God is watching you and, like a parent who walks behind a child, He is there to protect and help. Don't give up. Keep walking.

3

The Right Fit

Anybody who has ever worn tight shoes knows that nothing is more painful than having your feet cramped into a pair of shoes that do not fit. Even if you have never worn a pair of tight shoes, you might have experienced the discomfort of being in a garment that made you uncomfortable because the size or style did not quite match your needs. Walking in tight shoes is not only uncomfortable, but it can cause injuries, so most of us take special care in selecting the shoes we walk in and the clothes we wear because we want to be comfortable and we do not want to cause any harm to ourselves. Clothes and shoes that are too big are also avoided. We automatically shop for what suits us best because we consider the right fit to be important. The **right fit** is also essential in many aspects of life. In our Christian walk, it is particularly important that the vocation we choose, the strategies we employ to achieve our goals and the people we associate with be the right fit.

Strategies that Fit

One of the most compelling illustrations in the Bible of the importance of matching strategy with self is found in the story of David and Goliath (1 Samuel chapter 18). David was presented with Saul's armor, helmet, coat of mail and sword to go against Goliath in battle but he could not walk with them. "So David took them off" (1 Samuel 17:39 NKJV). That one sentence encapsulates my theory. The items David rejected were considered essential for battle but to David they were hindrances to success. He could not walk with them.

When we have a job to do it is important that we are familiar and comfortable with the approach we take. Some strategies might be deeply embedded in the culture of your organization but you need to employ the approach that matches your experience and purpose. David was experienced in the use of his sling and his ultimate purpose was to give glory to the Living God. David's confidence was not in his sling and stones; his confidence was in his God. Strategies that fit strengthen your faith in God and glorify His name.

Do not be Unequally Yoked

God expects us to nurture our relationships and do our best to care for those we love. 1 Peter 4:8 says, "And above all things have fervent love for one another, for "love will cover a multitude of sins". The word of God also admonishes us to forgive and keep on forgiving so our relationship with those around us should not be taken lightly or dispensed with easily. However, there are times when a relationship, even a blood relationship, becomes a danger to our Christian growth and it is necessary to sever ties with the individual or individuals who threaten our walk with God.

Here are five ways to tell when it is time to cut ties with someone:

- You never seem to agree on anything
- Their advice contradicts the word of God
- Being in their company makes you anxious or irritated
- You are the object of constant verbal or physical assault from the person
- The individual makes unreasonable demands on your time and resources

Any one of the situations listed above is reason to evaluate your relationship and determine whether or not you are unequally yoked. In 2 Corinthians 6:14, we are admonished, "Do not be unequally yoked together with unbelievers" This admonition extends to every type of alliance we are likely to enter. Discord, even danger, may be the result when people do not share the same principles in life. When there is discord, there is need for distance.

Genesis Chapter 13 chronicles the separation of Abram and Lot, uncle and nephew, indicating clearly that, sometimes, it is necessary to separate oneself, even from blood relatives. Abram and Lot had journeyed together and had been living in unity for many years, but the time had come when the two households were no longer dwelling in peace. Abram, very wisely, proposed that they go in separate directions. In life, as we experience personal growth, or the people we care about change in unpleasant ways, we may find it necessary to sever ties. I can hear you saying that we can't just discard people the way we discard shoes and clothes. You're right. However, there are times when it is absolutely necessary to put some distance between you and the individual or individuals who threaten your spiritual wellbeing.

Not being in close proximity does not necessarily mean that you cease to care about an individual. On the contrary, it may mean that you care about them too much to remain close to them, when closeness may result in the total destruction of your relationship. Abram and Lot put physical distance between the two households but, evidently, Abram still cared a lot about Lot. He was ready and willing to invest his time and resources to rescue Lot when Lot found himself in captivity. No doubt, Abram continued to love Lot and care about his wellbeing. They just needed to love each other from a distance. You, too, can love a relative or friend from a distance.

Severing Ties

There are times, though, when it is in your best interest to sever ties with an individual, just as you would discard a pair of tight shoes. In proverbs 1:10, young people are instructed to avoid people who encourage them to do wrong. If you want to stay on the path to eternal life, you have to be prepared to make some difficult decisions. You might encounter a situation in which, though horribly painful, you have to disassociate from someone or a group of people. Never hang on to alliances and occupations that impede your spirituality, choke your integrity, stifle your creativity, or crush your dreams of a better, brighter life. I want to encourage you to do some deep reflection and boldly eliminate from your life those things – vocation, partnerships, people, activities, whatever – which are a danger to your Christian walk.

While I was writing this chapter, I recalled an experience that was shared by a notable leader in the Caribbean. The leader shared his experience, which I am about to relate, at a lecture which I attended. He recounted how, when he was a boy, his mother had bought him a pair of shoes so that he could look his best on the day he wrote his qualifying exams for high school. He told his very captive audience how happy he was to have new shoes and how grateful he was to his mom for caring so much about how he looked on that important day. But, there was a problem. The shoes were a half size small. Now, in those days, merchandise was not returned to stores on various pretexts as they are today. The leader's mother had bought the pair of shoes and he was compelled to keep it and wear it.

Since hard earned cash had been spent for the shoes and the boy's mother would not have her boy, whom she was very proud of, attend that crucial exam in his bare feet, which is how he was used to attending school, he donned his tight shoes and journeyed to the town to write his examination. He recalled how, early in the exam, he realised he had to make a decision. It was either he endured the blistering pain of his tight shoes and fail his exam or take them off so that he could focus his attention on his assessment. He wrote his Eleven Plus Exam in his bare feet and today he credits the course of his life to that decision to take off his tight shoes.

You may not be enduring the pain of literal tight shoes, nor the discomfort of tight underwear, but is there a person or people in your life that you know you should get rid of? Are you engaged in a job or pastime that is injurious to your ultimate goal, that of achieving eternal life in Jesus? The relationship or occupation might have been perfect once but now you have come to realise it no longer fits. What will you do?

Let me hasten to state that the idea of severing ties should never extend to dropping dear, loyal friends just because you are now on a higher social rung than they are or you're now earning more and they are still stuck with the same net amount. I am referring to relationships that threaten your spiritual growth. Furthermore, I am not suggesting that you be hostile to those who do not profess to be Christians or ostracize people you once loved. The idea is for you to reflect on your relationships and ask God for guidance on how you should proceed. Perhaps, God will use you to change the heart of those who are moving in a different direction to you.

Your activities could also be a stumbling block that could potentially keep you out of God's kingdom. If your occupation leads you to spurn the will of God, make light of his commandments, then you are in danger. Now is the time to consider your daily activities on your job. With whom are you walking? What about your leisure activities or hobbies? Think carefully about whether or not the way you spend your time is promoting your development as a child of God. Your most important action in uncertainty is to consult the One who cares so much for you that He sent His Son to secure your eternal destiny. Proverbs 3:6 has this instruction: **In all your ways acknowledge Him, and He shall direct your paths** (NKJV). Let God be your guide.

The longer you stay in tight shoes, the more damage you do to yourself. Similarly, the longer you hold on to relationships or occupations that injure your spiritual development, the deeper will be the wounds you have to heal. You may even lose your life for holding on to relationships that do not support the direction in which you are headed.

Changing direction takes courage. It may appear to be easier or more expedient to maintain the status quo so we rationalise our alliances rather than face the hardship of justifying a change or adjusting to a new state without the individual or individuals in our lives. It may be that the individual or occupation is adding something to your life that you feel you cannot live without like financial security, material comfort or social recognition but deep in your heart, you know that the relationship/s are not the right fit for you because you cannot be your best self with that individual or occupation.

The bottomline is this: You just have to do some introspection and ask yourself where you are heading. What are your goals in life? Will your present situation hinder or enable your progress? I know it is not easy to leave friends behind, stop doing something that brings pleasure or resign from a job in which you have invested time and energy. However, if you are to fulfil your God appointed purpose in life, you have to make hard decisions and trust God to bring you to your Canaan.

"Be strong and of good courage, do not fear nor be afraid of them; for the Lord your God He is the One who goes with you. he will not leave you nor forsake you" (Deuteronomy 31:6, NKJV) Be kind to yourelf. Kick off your tight shoes.

4

Bold Appeals

Courage is an essential quality for the Christian in these times. When we are courageous, it shows because we cannot claim to be courageous and be silent in the face of injustice and blatant disregard for the law of God. We cannot claim to be courageous, and mute ourselves when the will of God is replaced by the will of man. There are countless situations in this terrible world that requires the Christian to fight for what is right. God expects us to defend the defenceless; He expects us to stand up for what we believe; He expects us to walk in light.

Making an Appeal

There are many things about cricket that I like - among them are the spectacular catches, the sensational sixes, the effervescent expressions of cricketers and spectators when a wicket falls - but nothing intrigues me more than a cricketer making an appeal. Invariably, the appeal is made by the bowler or wicket keeper so loudly and so boldly that, slim though the evidence may be, for the few moments that follow, players, spectators, viewers and listeners are caught in a theatrical pause. Once the cricketer believes he has gotten his opponent out, he stays firm until the third eye confirms his position or proves him wrong. Even then, sometimes, his body language suggests that he is relenting for the sake of the game and his team, but he still stands by his appeal. The attitude of a cricketer making an appeal is, in my opinion, worth emulating.

Standing up for Truth

In Romans 12:18 which reads, "If it is possible, as much as depends on you, live peaceably with all men", we are instructed that our actions should be governed by the principle of living peaceably with ALL men. This means that we should never knowingly create strife or a situation from which a war, verbal or otherwise, ensues. Conflict, though, is inevitable in life and, as Christians, seeking to be like Jesus, we have to be prepared to confront wrong boldly. It is honourable to stand up for what we believe. We cannot join the ranks of those who compromise what God expects of us to accommodate the shifting values of sinful man. Our greatest allegiance is to God. Not even the threat of death should cause us to waver. In 2 Timothy 1:7, we are assured, "For God has not given us a spirit of fear, but of power and of love and of a sound mind" (NKJV). So, when governments pass laws that violate what we know to be right in the sight of God, we have to defy them and echo the three Hebrew boys who dared to declare, "Our God whom we serve is able to deliver us" (Dan 3: 17, NKJV). We should never compromise when it comes to our allegiance to God. Emulate Joshua who announced to his fellow Israelites, "And if it seems evil to you to serve the Lord, choose for yourselves this day whom you will serve... But as for me and my house, we will serve the Lord" (Joshua 24:15, NKJV). Once we take a stand, we should continue fighting until the matter we are standing for is resolved. In this dark world, in these dangerous times, the matter may remain unchanged but we should continue to make strident appeals like a passionate cricketer.

Changing Course

Sometimes, (and this is not a contradiction of what I said earlier) as we journey on, we may discover that we are, in fact, in error or the actions we plan to take may have negative consequences. In these circumstances, we must change course. That is not only honourable, but wise. It is especially so when we are persuaded that we are not representing God in our current position. Too often, we hold on tenaciously to a position because we refuse to listen to reason or we just want to 'save face'. This, to my mind, is cowardly and utterly foolish. We can learn from the story of Abigail, David and Nabal that is recorded in 1Samuel 25. David was intent on destroying Nabal and his entire household because of Nabal's selfishness and insults to David's followers but this would not have been God's will. Abigail intervened, entreated

David to rethink his decision and David listened. Sometimes, standing up in the face of injustice requires us to relent from our natural inclinations to engage in physical battles. We should always consider the long term consequences of our actions as Abigail proposed to David that he should when he was bent on completely annihilating Nabal and everyone connected to him.

The Importance of Listening

Integral to my position - when you are right, stand your ground; make a bold appeal for justice and righteousness - is the importance of listening. Listening and, in fact, thinking critically are crucial elements in the process of getting conflicts resolved. When you listen critically, you pay attention to the literal and inferential meaning of what you are listening to. As a Christian, you evaluate the messages you receive in light of the principles of God's word. When messages conflict with what you believe, be considerate of the source's background. Think about the experiences that might have led the individual to hold the views that conflict with the principles you espouse and gently, compassionately, seek to shed light. Sometimes, it is unnecessary to give a verbal response to the messages we receive. Let our actions do the talking. The story of how Jesus dealt with the accusers of the woman who was caught in adultery is very instructive for us. In John 8:1-10 we read:

> But Jesus went to the Mount of Olives.
>
> [2] Now early in the morning He came again into the temple, and all the people came to Him;

and He sat down and taught them. [3] Then the scribes and Pharisees brought to Him a woman caught in adultery. And when they had set her in the midst, [4] they said to Him, "Teacher, this woman was caught in adultery, in the very act. [5] Now Moses, in the law, commanded us that such should be stoned. But what do You say?" [6] This they said, testing Him, that they might have something of which to accuse Him. But Jesus stooped down and wrote on the ground with His finger, as though He did not hear.

[7] So when they continued asking Him, He raised Himself up and said to them, "He who is without sin among you, let him throw a stone at her first." [8] And again He stooped down and wrote on the ground. [9] Then those who heard it, being convicted by their conscience, went out one by one, beginning with the oldest even to the last. And Jesus was left alone, and the woman standing in the midst.

Standing up for right implies that we are standing up to someone or a group; making an appeal requires an audience. To achieve our purpose, it is important that we know our audience and tailor our communication so that it has maximum effect.

Regardless of the issue or situation, be it social, economic, environmental or political, national or international, we have to stand up for what is right and do so fearlessly. Remember, you are never alone in any fight. In Isaiah 41:10 God gives us this assurance:

Fear not, for I *am* with you; Be not dismayed, for I *am* your God. I will strengthen you, Yes, I will help you, I will uphold you with My righteous right hand.

So, walk in love. Listen critically and make bold appeals.

5

Wanted: Breeze

Life is full of spectacular wonders that tell of the glory and wonder of God but how often do we pause to think about them? In this chapter, I will draw our attention to one of those wonders: breeze. Have you ever dwelt on what a remarkable blessing breeze is? Some time ago, I found myself in a situation in which my personal need for breeze was dramatically highlighted. Certainly, the coolness of gentle breeze is universally desirable but in the situation which I refer to, it hit me that our need for breeze is not uniform and our reaction to a lack of it or too much of it is markedly idiosyncratic.

I was a member of a group of people who had assembled in a room to complete a specific task over a period of days. A few members of the group that I was a part of quietly accepted the lack of breeze entering the inadequately ventilated room in which we were supposed to be mentally engaged and productive for several hours of each day. Quiet acceptance was the exception. The majority of my colleagues vociferously expressed their dissatisfaction with the lack of breeze which they pointed out would heighten their discomfort and make the task we were engaged in completely onerous.

Before long, we were shifting rooms, shifting furniture and vying for a place closest to the windows. Our attitudes varied significantly, determined by our perceived or actual need for breeze. Our desire for breeze, I mused, was yet another aspect of our uniqueness.

Over the next few days, I thought of what a remarkable and generally unappreciated blessing breeze is. Certainly, breeze is an emphatic revelation of God's creative wonder. The air that surrounds us is an aspect of creation and God designed it for a purpose. Whether we experience breeze, gale, storm or thunderstorm, we ought to remember that God is always in control. No element of nature operates outside the will of God.

Air and individuality

As I pondered on the idea that there are so many dimensions to my individuality, I started to think of the idiomatic expressions involving breeze and the positive symbolism of breeze in the English language. I am sure we could list several of these expressions. In all of them "breeze" has one element- ease. Because I am an educator and certainly because I was correcting Caribbean Secondary Education Certificate (CSEC) English A examination scripts at the time I referred to above, I thought about students. I mused that, from the perspective of a student, "breeze" was absolutely desirable because every student's desire is to be able to say on completion of an examination, "That was a breeze!" or "I just breezed through that paper!"

My musing continued over a period of days. I moved from thinking how desirable breeze was and how much we all appreciate ease of effort in every situation to how counterproductive too much ease and comfort could be. The last thing a teacher wants is to make her lessons so easy that her students are not challenged and they become bored and uninterested. In life, we need breeze but too much breeze for too long could hinder progress.

The dangers of heavy wind – gales, cyclones, typhoons, hurricanes - whatever bulldozing system we experience in the various regions of the world - are well documented. So, too, are the actions of mankind that contribute to boiling temperatures and more ferocious systems. Destructive winds clearly demand that we do our best to take care of the planet but, ultimately, God is in control of what we experience. The Bible (Jeremiah 4:11) makes a distinction between scorching wind and gentle blowing breeze, contrasting the effects of the two levels of force in the movement of air. While breeze is desirable, heavy winds are not. Scorching winds, though, actual and symbolic, have a role in human development.

Refreshed, not Blown Over

Extending the metaphor to the existence of ease and hardships in the life of a Christian, I thought of how much God uses this element to reassure us of His love. In our walk, God allows us to enjoy blessings that are beautiful and refreshing but He also allows us to experience the gales of strife and struggle. He would never allow us to be blown over but it is only when we struggle that we truly appreciate the power of God to restore calm and peace to our lives. When God allows us to struggle, His intention is to rid us of those traits that will restrict our worship. Sometimes, a heavy gust of strife is what we need to shake us up and make us reach for him in faith. God is our deliverer. He is the one who sustains us in every situation. We have to learn to trust Him when we are buffeted by heavy winds, as well as when we are breezing through life.

Provide Breeze for Others

On our Christian journey, we would do well to consider how God reminds us of His love every time we feel the coolness of breeze. We also need to consider how we interact with those around us. What kind of experience do we provide for those we have to deal with? As parent, teacher, coach, administrator, doctor, pastor, politician, explorer or reporter, every one of us needs to regularly assess whether the experiences we provide are refreshing and enabling, or whether we are guilty of ripping away pieces of the people we are positioned to serve. If we follow God's instruction to love our neighbours as ourselves, we would be breeze to those around us.

Remember, too, that the force of wind that uproots one tree or rips the roof off of one building might just bend the branches of another tree or raise the galvanize from the beam of a roof. People do not uniformly relate to experiences but whatever their individual needs and reactions are, we all have one thing in common. We all desire a certain amount of ease, I mean "breeze", to keep us happy and functioning at our best. So, praise God for breeze and ask him to help us make life more pleasant for those we interact with.

6

Cherish your Dreams

We should all have dreams that we cherish. Dreams give us the drive to wake up and reach out to God in faith that He will honour His words in John 16:24: "Until now you have asked nothing in My name. Ask, and you will receive, that your joy may be full" (NKJV). Let God help you to realise your dreams. What am I talking about here? I speak of dreams that are synonymous with hopes, aspirations and desires to achieve more, to progress beyond our current position in every aspect of our lives. If you don't have a dream, you should create one. The pursuit of your dream provides a compelling reason to get up in the morning. Dreams are, to life, like the green matter in a leaf. If you cease to dream, you may just lose the essence of living.

Your Dreams Versus God's Will

We should have hopes and aspirations, but as Christians, we have to remember that God has a plan for each of our lives so our aspirations should be consistent with God's will for our lives and the gifts he has granted us. Service to God ought to be central to our aspirations. Jeremiah 1:5 states, "**Before I formed you** in the womb **I** knew **you; Before you** were born **I** sanctified **you; I** ordained **you** a prophet to the nations." (NKJV) We know from Jeremiah's experience that God has a plan and a purpose for each of our lives, so seek His guidance and direction when you are dreaming. Do not dream of being a 21st century Beethoven when God has ordained you to be a Picasso. In the body of Christ, what we aspire to be and do is subject to what God has called us to do. 1 Corinthians 12: 4 declares, "There are diversities of gifts, but the same Spirit. There are differences of ministries, but the same Lord. And there are diversities of activities, but it is the same God who works all in all." Don't aspire to be what God did not design you to be.

Jeremiah 29:11 says, "For I know the thoughts that I think toward you, says the Lord, thoughts of peace and not of evil, to give you a future and a hope." Our dream may not be what God has mapped out for us but we can be certain that God's plan is always perfect. So, whatever your dream is, commit it to God. If it is what He has ordained for you, it will come to fruition. "Commit your works to the Lord, and your thoughts will be established" (**Proverbs 16:3**).

Hold Fast In Spite of Challenges

In pursuit of your dreams, you may have to climb mountains and cross valleys, but cherish your dreams enough to never let them go. No matter what difficulties you encounter, remember you are admonished not to be anxious about anything, but in every situation, by prayer and petition, with thanksgiving, present your requests to God (Philippians 4:6). If you truly cherish your dream, you would certainly 'hold fast' to it. On my doctoral journey, I experienced many personal challenges. I developed an eye condition and had to undergo surgery, my mother passed away and losing her threw me into an abyss of grief, I had challenges at home that diverted my focus, the supervisors I began the journey with left the university, and I can go on and on to list the many obstacles that emerged to block my path. But I knew, that the knowledge and experience I would gain from completing my doctoral programme would enrich my life so I held on. There were times that I was discouraged but I never considered quitting. I wanted to complete the programme and I knew that with God's help, I would, even if it took me longer than I expected. Now that I have successfully completed my doctoral degree, I can say, confidently, that every delay was permitted by God for a purpose. How much we cherish our dreams will determine the height of the waves we dare to ride, the mountains we climb, the rivers we cross and the ditches we boldly step into and emerge from.

As followers of Christ, we are expected to enjoy the best things in life; Jesus himself said, "The thief does not come except to steal, and to kill, and to destroy. I have come that they may have life, and that they may have it more abundantly" (John 10:10, NKJV). So, dream big and hold fast to your dream.

Your Dream, your Personal Constellation

For the world, the admonition to 'dream big' is, more often than not, a "one size fits all" charge. It is invariably synonymous with making a lot of money. We should all dream big; but a big dream doesn't necessarily mean getting rich or making any money at all. Your dream should be uniquely about you and God's will for your life. As far as dreams go, my Hydra might be your Crux, not the same size but still incredibly magnificent. Do not compare your dream to anyone else's. Your dream is your personal constellation, a pattern that is uniquely yours. Every man, woman and child should always be relentlessly pursuing a dream, aspiring to something, hoping for something, striving to achieve something. That something, though, should be consistent with one's personal growth and development. You should strive to shine brightly where you are situated and glorify God with the blessings He has bestowed upon you.

The Most Significant Aspiration

While we strive for accomplishments on earth, we should bear in mind the admonition of Ecclesiastes 12:13-14, "Let us hear the conclusion of the whole matter: Fear God and keep His commandments, For this is man's all. 14 For God will bring every work into judgment, Including every secret thing, Whether good or evil" (NKJV). Our greatest aspiration, our greatest dream should be a rich relationship with God. Everything on earth is transient so the only thing that truly matters is spiritual growth. The admonition we are given in Romans 12:2 constrains the dreams of true Christians: "And do not be conformed to this world, but be transformed by the renewing of your mind, that you may prove what is that good and acceptable and perfect will of God" (NKJV). This is what adds energy to life, creates dynamism and keeps us forging forward. Like the apostle Paul, we should always be pressing forward to the most important goal which is to fulfil the perfect will of God. In Philippians 3:14 he declares, "I press toward the goal for the prize of the upward call of God in Christ Jesus."

Yet, our goal of living Christ-like lives should not prevent us from striving for success here. There is a difference between doing our best in every situation, setting high standards for ourselves and being obsessed with glory on earth. After all, God expects us to live abundant lives. He expects us to 'dream big'. Once our hopes and dreams are consistent with God's will for our lives, we will prosper if we aspire to be the best of what we are called to be. God expects us to be diligent. Proverbs 12:24 assures us that diligence brings positive results. It says, "The hand of the diligent will rule, but the lazy *man* will be put to forced labor". We would make a marvellous difference in the world if we were passionate about fulfilling our God appointed purpose AND doing the very best we could in every situation. What's your cherished dream? Is it God's will for your life? If you have the assurance that it is, then pursue it with all your might.

7

Favoured Colour

How do you relate to people of other ethnicities, particularly people of a different colour? One of the greatest challenges facing the world today, is the integration of people of different ethnicities. The church is not exempt from this challenge. I always marvel at how white, brown or yellow Christian congregations are even in communities where people of different ethnic groups reside. At some point in your Christian walk, you will be confronted with the issue of colour. What will be your true response?

Many of us have a favourite colour or favourite colours. Our preferences may be so strong that even casual acquaintances note the dominance of our favoured colour in our wardrobe and among our personal artifacts. Our choice of hue or tint may be based on the general symbolism of the colour or what it means to us personally. Whatever the reason for the preference, our choices constitute part of what makes us all special. Have you ever noticed that when people are gathered in a room and an item in different colours is being shared, people invariably voice their preference for one colour or another? "I'd like the red one," someone might say, while another reaches for the green item. There is no shame in that. Each person has the privilege of choice and each person's choice is usually respected. Differences in selections seldom give rise to anything more than good-natured bantering. Having a favourite colour in the sense of hue or tint is quite harmless so it is readily revealed. In contrast, the idea of a "favourite colour" when colour signifies race, nationality, ethnic group, religion or tribe is not as readily disclosed, but it manifests itself in bigotry, intolerance, and even acts of hatred.

When people hate other people, they tend to degenerate into inhumane behaviour. History records that some of the worst atrocities of human history were committed because one group of people, defined by race, nationality, ethnicity, religion or political views, hated another. This is a reality that, as Christians, we cannot ignore. Because we profess to be followers of Christ, many of us try to conceal how we truly feel about people of different races and nationalities. Yet, we convey through subtle or not so subtle messages, in our words and actions, our inner feelings. Search your heart. Where do you stand on this issue?

Christians and Intolerance

Intolerance has no place among Christians. When people shamelessly favour one human group above another, we must join the ranks of those who condemn their actions. We must do all we can to promote acceptance, love and unity. Romans 12:10 admonishes us to "Be kindly affectionate to one another with brotherly love, in honor giving preference to one another" (NKJV). No Christian should have a favourite colour when "colour" means race, nationality, ethnic group or gender and by gender I mean male and female as created by God and established for eternity in Genesis 1:27 which reads, "So God created man in His own image; in the image of God He created him; male and female He created them" (NKJV). Yet, regardless of what post-Eden gender label people adopt, we are called upon as Christians to love the whole world.

The vehement rejection of other "colours" betrays trust, destroys friendships, engenders hate, divides people and destroys lives. To counter these destructive consequences, each race, nationality, ethnic group, gender, religion and political ideology ought to be given equal opportunities in every situation. Equal opportunity is a fundamental principle that we should never be silent about if we truly believe every human being is of equal value. This is not to say that there are not important differences and fundamental strengths in various groupings but these are no grounds for elevating one group above another. Embracing our differences and valuing all our strengths engenders growth. Countless opportunities for creative synergies are lost when we separate and isolate because of our differences. Unity offers valuable opportunities to celebrate our diversity and achieve great things.

Political and Religious Divisions

Globally, political and religious ideology seem to be the most divisive choices that people make. Differences of race, nationality, and ethnic group seem to dissipate under political and religious banners and often, so does common sense. What is the benefit of hating your fellowmen because they espouse opposing political or religious views? Rejection and hatred of others because of the views they hold erodes the possibility of sharing and celebrating what we have in common. It is unjustifiable. We must bear in mind that it is the same God who created all mankind, the same God who sustains all mankind, the same God who loves the whole world so perfectly that he sent his son to die for it. John 3:16 says, "For God so loved the world that He gave His only begotten Son, that whoever believes in Him should not perish but have everlasting life." Furthermore, we have to remember that God is always in control of the affairs of men and it is He who permits leaders to rise and fall. In Daniel 4:17, we are expressly told, "This decision *is* by the decree of the watchers, And the sentence by the word of the holy ones, In order that the living may know That the Most High rules in the kingdom of men, Gives it to whomever He will, And sets over it the lowest of men."

Admittedly, some groups hold views and make choices that are harmful to the collective good of society. The headlines abound with the heinous crimes that are committed under the banner of beliefs but even those people ought to be loved. The great Mahatma Gandhi is credited with the words, *"Whenever you are confronted with an opponent, conquer him with love"*. Rather than violent verbal or physical assaults on political and religious opponents, we should seek to win them over with kindness and reason.

God's Will for Mankind

When we observe nature, it is evident that God has prepared clear guidance for us on the subject of diversity. In the sky above and here on earth, in furs and feathers, fruits and flowers, the azure sea and metals rare, God's love of colour is so clear. In His wisdom, he created a marvellous variety to enrich our lives and teach us to appreciate diversity. I believe this is particularly true when colour equals race, nationality or ethnic group.

If I were to ask, "what's your favourite colour?" and mean, "what's your favourite nationality, ethnic group or race, what would your answer be? Would you actually have a selection to name? Think about it, is such a choice justifiable? My view is that there is no logical basis for human beings to exclusively favour one race, nationality or ethnic group above others. There are situations such as in an olympic competition when choices have to be made but these choices should be based on merit and not on favour. We should never choose a competitor merely because the individual is one race or another, one nationality or another or one ethnic group or another. Our belief in creation and the origin of the world should lead to our belief in the brotherhood of man. There are only two groups in God's eyes: those who serve him and those who do not. He expects those who serve Him to demonstrate his love to those who do not so that they too can come to know and love the God of all creation. Jesus Christ came and died so that 'whosoever' of whatever, race or nationality, who believes in him can be saved. "Beloved, if God so loved us, we ought also to love one another" (1 john 4:11, NKJV).

Let's love our fellowmen. It would make our walk so much more joyful. Our shared humanity transcends all our differences. Let's celebrate our diversity and strive to live in harmony.

8

On Efforts and Expectations

God allows us to have various experiences to help us grow in grace and fulfil his mandate while we journey on in these last days. One of the messages in God's word that should be etched in our minds is found in Psalm 32:8 which says, "I will instruct you and teach you in the way you should go; I will guide you with My eye" Every experience should be viewed as God's instruction to us and we should seek to learn from even mundane everyday occurrences. Here's an experience that taught me four significant lessons. I had had similar experiences in the past but on this occasion, unlike the previous occasions on which I had this interesting experience, I allowed myself to dwell on the symbolism of what may be dismissed as an insignificant, random occurrence. Through this experience, I believe God was reminding me of the important principle of ensuring that effort and expected outcome are aligned.

Missing a Desirable fruit

I was picking mangoes from a tree in my backyard. Hanging from a branch at least five feet beyond my unaided reach was a mature, deliciously sun-kissed mango that was perfect for my pre-breakfast palate. I definitely had to pick that mango. It was clearly ready to be liberated from the company of noticeably green fruit that surrounded it.

However, I had a problem. I do not own a fruit picker. That simple, yet ingenious, invention would have made it easy for me to cradle the desirable fruit and, with a firm yank, separate the half pound Julie sweetness from the small, solidly green mangoes around it. Unfortunately, for no particular reason, I have never acquired a fruit picker. The three-foot long stick that was helping me to pick the single seed, vitamin rich fruit was too short to reach the mango I wanted to pick. Nevertheless, I was not about to leave that particular mango to the eager pecking of blackbirds and kiskadees. I wanted it, and I was going to get it. I put too much value on the fibre, vitamins C, A and B6 that mangoes provide to allow the neighnourhood birds to beat me to this one. Without taking the time to consider my options, I made my move. I leapt. I grabbed the lower end of the branch. I gave it a vigorous shake. To my dismay, green mangoes came tumbling down, but the succulent fruit, the one I expected to slip easily from its stem, remained on the tree. Despite my energetic shake, I had not succeeded in dislodging the fruit I wanted from its position.

Making Disciples

Instantly, I realised that there were object lessons to be learnt from this experience. Before Jesus ascended to heaven, His disciples were assembled together "And Jesus came and spoke to them, saying, "All authority has been given to Me in heaven and on earth. Go therefore and make disciples of all the nations, baptizing them in the name of the Father and of the Son and of the Holy Spirit, teaching them to observe all things that I have commanded you; and lo, I am with you always, *even* to the end of the age." (Matthew 28:18-20, NKJV). Jesus expects us to make disciples and we may go out expending great effort to do just that but fail to obtain the desired fruit. My experience with trying to pick the mango I wanted is a demonstration of what could potentially result when the effort or strategies we employ are dissonant with the goal or outcome we expect. Our efforts, the steps we take, the actions we perform must align with what we hope to achieve.

When we are targeting particular individuals for discipleship, we have to be careful that our efforts are not in vain. There are four key principles that we should note:

1. First, we must consider the environment of our target group. If we are not careful about how we enter the environment, we may fail to reach our target and we may destroy any prospect of later success with other individuals in that environment.

2. Secondly, we should carefully consider the strategy we intend to apply in reaching persons. Though the goal of making disciples of all men is a noble one, if we apply the wrong strategy, take the wrong course of action,

adopt an inappropriate approach, we may never achieve our goal.

3. We should not be hasty. Had I taken the time to consider alternative approaches, I would have realised that yanking a branch full of mangoes that were not ready to be picked to get one ripe mango was not the best course of action.

4. When our efforts fail to give us the expected results, we should try again.

Following Jesus' example

Jesus showed us, clearly, that different approaches are needed in dealing with individuals. He healed many persons during his ministry on earth using a variety of strategies. To some, he gave a healing touch, to others, he spoke gently and yet others, he befriended and they experienced transformation through their interaction with him. Jesus set us an example of knowing the circumstances of an individual's life when we are approaching them with the good news of salvation. My hapless experience of the fallen green mangoes and the unpicked ripe mango suggests to me that, sometimes, appearances may suggest that someone is ready to receive the gospel, and maybe the person is ready, but the approach we use leaves the individual untouched. It also suggests that we may overlook people who are ready to be 'picked' for God's kingdom because outwardly, they don't seem to be ready. The green mangoes which I expected to remain firmly attached to their stems came tumbling down while the ripe mango remained firmly in place.

Roles and Readiness

This analogy can also be applied when we are selecting individuals to fulfil roles in the church. The youth or those who cannot boast of a long walk with the Lord might be overlooked in favour of older, 'riper' individuals but we should always remember that God selected Joseph, the second to last of Jacob's sons to save his people from famine. He also selected David, the youngest of Jesse's sons to be king of Israel because "The Lord does not see as man sees; for man looks at the outward appearance, but the Lord looks at the heart." (1 Samuel 16:7, NKJV). So, be mindful of dismissing persons who are ready to serve because they don't seem 'ripe'.

After the green mangoes came tumbling down, I remonstrated over my wasted effort for a few moments and then I went in search of something else to help me pick the mango. Very soon, I came across a one-inch PVC pole that was long enough to reach the mango. I position it directly under the ripened fruit and pushed. As soon as the pole connected with the mango, it slipped from the stem. Just like that. With the right tool, it took very little effort for me to get the ripe mango. Jesus instructs us to make disciples of all men; He expects us to use the right approach in every situation.

9

The Pure Milk of the Word

Milk is said to be a complete food. It has all the nutrients one needs to develop and stay strong. It is very appropriate, therefore, for it to be used as a metaphor for the scriptures. In 1 Peter 2:1-2, the followers of Christ are admonished to "desire the pure milk of the word". Desire is a strong verb. It denotes a deep craving. As Christians, we are instructed to have a deep longing for the word of God. This longing for the scriptures is motivated by the understanding that the only way to make it to the end of this journey is to delve into the word of God regularly. Our lives have to be guided by the principles that God has given us to live by. 2 Timothy 3:16-17 informs us that, "All scripture is given by inspiration of God, and is profitable for doctrine, for reproof, for correction, for instruction in righteousness: That the man of God may be perfect, thoroughly furnished unto all good works" (NKJV). From Genesis to Revelation, God's word is packed with what we need to sustain us on this journey.

Purity of the Scriptures

The sixty-six books of the Bible were written by people of various stations in life who lived in different eras but every line was inspired by God. While Bible commentaries are influenced by the beliefs which the writers espouse, the Bible provides an infallible representation of what God wants us to know, understand and apply to our lives. The Bible explains itself and God grants wisdom to those who earnestly seek Him through His word. While Bible commentaries are useful, they should not be substitutes for the Bible. Every Christian must engage in earnest personal study of God's word. Some people ignore parts of the Bible because they falsely believe that aspects of it are no longer relevant to us today. Jesus Himself said, "For assuredly, I say to you, till heaven and earth pass away, one jot or one tittle will by no means pass from the law till all is fulfilled" (Matthew 5:18, NKJV). Every sentence in the Bible is as relevant to us to today as it was when it was inspired.

Benefits of Studying the Word of God

Beyond the boundaries of our carnal mind, lie vistas of truth that can only be accessed through earnest study of God's word. As you delve into the Bible, the same Holy Spirit which inspired its authors will enlighten you. You will experience benefits that only God can provide. Many of the benefits you receive will be personal to you, but here are four that I believe are universal.

Avoidance of Sin

The Christian walk requires not just the reading of God's word but diligent study of the word, and consistent efforts to commit God's word into our hearts. Psalm 119:11 declares, "Your word I have **hidden in my heart**, that I might not sin against You". That's the ultimate purpose for storing God's word in our hearts. We hide God's word in our heart to avoid sinning against God. Sin is the transgression of God's law but if God's law is hidden in our hearts, then it will influence our thoughts and actions. Out of the abundance of our hearts, we will speak and act. We will live in accordance with what God expects of us.

Guidance for Life

God's word also sheds light. Many of the most enduring arguments that occupy our time, could be easily settled by following the "pure milk of the word". The Bible is very plain about the origin of life, and it provides us with an explicit record of earth's history so that there should be no doubt about where we came from, where we are now and where we are headed. Light dispels darkness, so without the word of God we will grope in darkness over key issues. Matters which perplex mankind such as marital relations, worship, family life, finance, gender, international relations, care for the environment and diet, would be quite straightforward if we followed the principles of God's word. In fact, every aspect of life can be guided by the word of God. It is no wonder the Psalmist declared, "Your word *is* a **lamp** to my feet and a **light** to my **path**" (Psalm 119:105, NKJV). When our path is lit, we can see where we are headed, we can avoid dangers that lie along the way and we can walk boldly with the assurance that even if we stumble, because we are walking in the light of God's word, we can get on our feet and keep moving.

Encouragement and Assurances

The study of the Bible provides encouragement and solid assurance of God's love. Life is challenging but we can live joyfully because of the promises of God. Just as there is guidance in the Bible for every facet of life, there is a promise for every situation. Are you burdened by the cares of this world? God invites you to be free from worry by "casting all your care upon Him, for He cares for you" (1 Peter 5:7, NKJV). What wonderful assurance! The same word tells us in Philipians 4:19 that "And my God shall supply all your need according to His riches in glory by Christ Jesus (NKJV). Whatever your need is, all you have to do is ask and it shall be given to you. God promises to supply all that we need and he is faithful. He fulfils His promises. All we have to do is trust Him.

Acquaintance with God

Perhaps the most important benefit we derive from studying God's word is getting more acquainted with God. All the other benefits contribute to this overarching benefit. The Bible is a transcript of God's character. By searching the scriptures, we come to know the God who is revealed in the scriptures. In Jeremiah 29:13 God says, "And you will seek Me and find *Me,* when you search for Me with all your heart" (NKJV) Where better to start searching for God but in His word? The sixty-six books of the Bible are a revelation of the great I AM. It is only through prayerful study that you can come to understand the God who "so loved the world that He gave His only begotten Son, that whoever believes in Him should not perish but have everlasting life" **(John 3:16, NKJV).**

Have you longed for the pure milk of the word? Just open your Bible and be filled.

10

Leading Under Threat

Are you a leader? You may not be the head of state, an executive in a major corporation, the head of a ministry or in charge of a department at your place of employment but in some sphere and to some degree, you are in charge. If there are people who depend on you for guidance or you have been placed in authority over a group of people and you have the responsibility of ensuring that common goals are met, you are functioning as a leader. You don't even have to hold a formal position of authority to lead. A leader influences others so if you are exerting any form of influence over others, you are leading. Perhaps, according to any current framework of effective leadership, you are outstanding. Your followers cooperate with you and what you have achieved is outstanding. You have a vision and you are making strides towards realising that vision. You might have put a sound structure to every process that you are responsible for, you show compassion, you share your responsibilities and you seek out avenues to empower those around you. You sincerely do everything you are capable of to ensure that your sphere of authority is free of anxiety and every member of your group can flourish. But, just when you think your leadership is prospering and you are satisfied that your country, your corporation, your ministry, your department, your family or your life is secure, you are faced with a threat. What do you do when someone or something tries to invade your space and your leadership is threatened?

Responding to Threats

Threat creates stress and we usually have two responses to stress. We either fight the source of our stress or we flee from it. It is the proverbial fight or flight response that is also accompanied by an increase in the stress hormone and multiple health risks if we are exposed to prolonged and repeated stressful conditions. When our leadership is threatened, our response may be a little more complicated. Some of us may panic and rush around trying to defend our position by appealing to those whom we consider to be our ardent supporters. We might eliminate the threat by getting persons fired, others may be petrified with fear. Still others may get angry and launch a counter-attack against everybody who so much as smell a little threatening. No doubt, you would wish to adopt some strategy to retain control of your authority. It is unlikely that you would meekly stand by and allow someone or something to oust you from your leadership position. Taking the right actions when your authority is threatened could be challenging but the Bible provides a strategy which I call *The Hezekiah Approach* that would ensure that you lead successfully and remain triumphant in the face of any threat.

The Hezekiah Approach

2 Chronicles 32:1-22 outlines the steps in the approach that I am advancing as a foolproof strategy for leading successfully and dealing with threats.

1. The first step is for you to be aware that threats are a part of life. Whether they come in the form of people, a disease or a new system, there will always be challenges that invade your space and seek to end your control.
2. Acknowledge the threat. Don't ignore challenges to your authority. You need to develop keen awareness of what is going on around you so that when a threat appears you will notice it.
3. Consult with your human capital and present obstacles that would make the task of who or what is threatening you difficult. Do not let people use your resources to get the better of you. You have to examine your situation and start "blocking off the water" (vs 3 NIV).
4. Strengthen your position by tightening any loopholes that would allow the threat to advance. If a disease is threatening your control, adopt a life-style that would halt or hinder its progress. You also need to create systems that would serve as a defense against

human threat. This may mean developing new skills or sharpening the skills you already possess. Whatever you do, ensure that you put yourself in a stronger position of authority than when the threat first appeared.

5. Delegate responsibilities. As a leader, you should be aware that you cannot be everywhere and do everything so you have to distribute your leadership by allowing others to take charge as well.

6. Communicate with those you lead and inspire them with confidence. This is a very important step in the Hezekiah approach to leading under threat. In fact, it is the zenith of the approach. Hezekiah was confident of his security. He was certain he would defeat Sennacherib, not only because of the systems he had put in place, but because of his assurance that "there is a greater power with us than with him. With him is only the arm of flesh but with us is the Lord our God to help us and to fight our battles" (vss 7-8). Notice that Hezekiah made the situation clear to his followers and he assured them of victory.

7. Acknowledge your source of strength. As a Christian, you should always express the confidence that your God is able to fight your battles and lead you to victory. Don't worry about individuals who are scheming to get you out of your position. They might have done it to others before and gotten away with it. They might have more experience and greater resources than you have but don't worry. They are already defeated. Believe it, express it and watch it come to pass.

8. Finally, pray fervently and get others to pray with you. Verses 20-22 provide the resolution of this threatening situation which King Hezekiah faced. He and the prophet Isaiah "cried out in prayer to heaven ... and the Lord sent an angel, who annihilated all the fighting men and the commanders and officers in the camp of the Assyrian king ... so the Lord saved Hezekiah" (Verses 20-23, NIV).

If you believe, the Lord will destroy any threat that you are faced with, but you have a part to play. The approach taken by Hezekiah when Sennacherib king of Assyria came and invaded Judah is a framework for successful leadership, especially in the face of a threat. Try it. Like Hezekiah, your leadership will be secure and others will regard you highly as a result.

11

Let it Rain!

Let it rain, let it rain, let it rain! When you are caught in a storm, let peace reign in your heart. Be still. Even if torrents come and creeks overflow, your rivers swell and ocean currents roll, be still. The God who set the rainbow in the sky, is always in control. You may feel the impact of the storm, but no storm can separate you from the love of God. This is the confidence that comes from holding on to the enduring promises that are stored in the Word of God. The earnest Christian can expect to experience inexplicable hardships in life. However, it is paramount that we adopt an attitude of praise in every situation. I Thessalonians 5:18 says, "in everything give thanks; for this is the will of God in Christ Jesus for you" (NKJV). God knows that we will have experiences that we would not naturally be thankful for so he was careful to include this admonition in the scriptures.

Dealing with inexplicable hardships

In 2 Timothy 3:12, we are told that "All who desire to live godly in Christ Jesus will suffer persecution" (NKJV). So, for us, it's not a matter of if but when hardships will come. How do you deal with your hardships? In seasons of torrential challenges, misfortunes, hardships - call them whatever you will, there's a tendency for us to feel as if we have been abandoned by God. The Psalms are replete with expressions that reveal the Psalmists' feelings of abandonment. In Psalm 13, David cries, "How long, O Lord? Will you forget me forever? How long will You hide Your face from me?" (Verse 1, NKJV) The Psalms are also filled with expressions of confidence that God is "Our refuge and strength, A very present help in trouble" (Psalm 46:1). Surely, there will be seasons of weeping and mourning but these seasons don't last forever. When you are buffeted by challenges, just trust the perfect will of God. After the weeping, there will be laughter. There will be mourning, but there will also be dancing. Wait patiently on the Lord and He will take you safely through the storm.

The Nature of Rain

Rain takes many forms. It may be the loss of a childhood friend or a loving spouse who suddenly departs this life. Your rain may be conflict at home or at work or even conflict in both of these domains. Marital issues are another form of rain and so are poor health, overdue bills that keep piling up, unemployment, and the waywardness of children. Yes, there may be torrential rainfall in your life but if there were no rain, there would be no growth. Our prayer, when we experience challenges on this journey should be:

Lord, let your will be done on earth as it is in heaven. Grant me peace during this time of trouble for I know that you are totally in control and you will dry my tears. I am trusting you because You have invited me to cast all my cares upon you because You care for me. I claim every promise that speaks to my situation and I give You all the praise, honour and glory for what You have done and will continue to do in my life.

Rain is an ideal symbol for misfortune or trouble. Just as rain can occur with varying intensity and last for unpredictable periods, so the word 'trouble' can be applied to a kaleidoscope of situations. A little 'trouble' with a sore thumb is certainly not the same as 'trouble' with the car, 'trouble' in a marriage or the kind of 'trouble' that comes when you have broken a civic law. No sensible person would call a drizzle, a downpour and keep a straight face; but, it's still rain. Whether it lasts for a few minutes, a couple of hours or days, rain is rain. When it comes to trouble, a little drizzle for someone may feel like a downpour for another person.

God Permits Every Hardship

Whatever the intensity of your hardship, you can be sure that God has allowed it because he knows you can handle it. This statement is practically a cliché in Christian circles but it is true. You cannot afford to lose your faith or question God's providence over a season of rain. Hardships refresh your Christian experience. Just as the rain washes away impurities and brightens the world, so will these experiences cleanse you of traits that hinder your walk with God. Spiritual growth germinate from challenges. Let it rain! The God of the sunshine is the God of the rain. If your life was just bare sunshine you'd wither and die. God knows what proportion of rain to pour into your life so that you can flourish and grow. Be grateful for every experience that God allows you to have. It is because He loves you and wants you to learn to trust Him more that He permits the hardships that you face.

As much as we know from Job's experience that some of our troubles may be orchestrated by the devil, we also know from Job's experience that the devil can only do to us what God allows him to do. On the authority of God's immutable word, there's a rainbow for every spell of rain that the devil showers on you. Just search the scriptures and fall to your knees, not in despair but to gather strength and to implore God for His guidance and mercy. He assures us in Isaiah 41:10, "Fear not, for I am with you; Be not dismayed, for I am your God. I will strengthen you, Yes, I will help you, I will uphold you with My righteous right hand" (NKJV).

Shelter in God's Promises

During your rainy season, find shelter in the promises of God. Remember that Jehovah is your hiding place, He will protect you from trouble and surround you with songs of deliverance (Psalm 32:7). Stand firmly on the belief that "all things work together for good to those who love God, to those who are called according to His purpose" (Romans 8:28). God will give you rest. You will be refreshed by His grace and bring forth abundant fruit but believe this: Abundant fruit comes after abundant rain.

12

Looking at Crises
Iguana Style

When man made or natural disasters strike, God always shows us that he cares. He may even use a simple reptile to remind us that His natural order reigns supreme. In the midst of the Corona Virus lockdown, an iguana – a large, rough- skinned, long-tailed lizard – appeared on my water tank, in the middle of the day, bringing with it a message of hope. When we spotted it, I was filled with wonder. Where did this creature appear from? I had never seen an iguana in my yard before but right then I realised a mystery had been solved.

That strange creature was the culprit who had robbed me of many juicy mangoes and delectable papaws (papayas). The one who caused me to exclaim with frustration when a fruit that I had been eyeing and waiting for the right time to pick, was found, while the grass was still wet from dew, almost completely devoured. It was a cunning foe. Blending perfectly with the trees, it had managed to evade detection before that morning. This four legged reptile was quite unlike the many keskidees, black birds, and doves which reside in and around my yard. It was not even a blink as welcome as the occasional hummingbird that I spot or the gaulin bird that feeds from my dog's pan. Birds just peck, and since I believe in the extra sweetness of a bird-pecked fruit, I don't mind the birds at all. But this creature leaves the fruit it selects useless. If the fruit is still hanging from the tree after an iguana has fed on it, I can only knock the remaining portion to the ground in disgust. So, for a few minutes, I wanted to destroy that iguana. It did not matter to me that it was clearly a young one judging from its length because iguanas can reach a total length of six feet. This one was just about one and a half feet long. I started to imagine how I would capture it and put an end to its wretched life.

God's Power to Provide

But then, my perspective shifted. It was if the Holy Spirit was instructing me and, suddenly, my attitude to that iguana changed. Yes, it eats my julie mangoes, it devours my papaws and my guavas but I had never seen it. Until that day it had escaped my attention. Why did God allow me to see it while the world was gripped by despair? Why, in the midst of world-wide death and destruction did I see it? I realised that young iguana was a symbol of hope, of industry, of God's creative power and certainly of God's power to provide. More importantly, it appeared, free and unmasked, while I was locked in because of Covid-19. I was certain God was reminding me that the reptiles were provided for, and **He certainly will provide for my needs**.

The Covid-19 pandemic was horrible, the disease still claims many lives but the natural order of the universe continues. Every crisis we face, personally, as a family, a nation, or on a global scale is subject to God's will. He owns everything. Psalm 50: 10-11 says, "For every beast of the forest is mine, And the cattle on a thousand hills. I know all the birds of the mountains, And the wild beasts of the field are Mine" (NKJV). That iguana that I wished to destroy belonged to God and He was providing for it. The appearance of that iguana underscored the truth that when God allows disasters to strike, reassuring symbols of his sovereignty always remain intact. We would do well to draw comfort and hope from observing nature. The sun rises in the morning and sets at dusk, the moon shines at night and stars bedeck the sky. All through the pandemic, the wind continued its distinctive serenade and I could feel its coolness just the same. I could smell the fragrance of flowers and admire their delicate loveliness. Animals were giving birth to their young; they fed and frolicked. All creatures sought food and wandered freely as they had always done. Truly, there is hope and beauty all around. Covid-19 cannot suppress that! God's promises stand firm in the midst of every crisis. Matthew 10: 28-30 says, "And do not fear those who kill the body but cannot kill the soul. But rather fear Him who is able to destroy both soul and body in [a]hell. Are not two sparrows sold for a copper coin? And not one of them falls to the ground apart from your Father's will. But the very hairs of your head are all numbered".

Change Your Perspective

The Bible has many passages that reassure us of God's undying love for us and His constant care during the crises of life. We, however, like Elijah, tend to lose sight of previous victories and panic when our lives and livelihood are threatened (1 Kings 19). Don't panic! Turn to God in times of Crisis. Psalm 50:15 declares, "Call upon Me in the day of trouble; I will deliver you, and you shall glorify Me." The text suggests that a day of trouble is inevitable. We can be certain that once we are alive there will be Ahabs and Jezebels who wish to destroy us because we are standing up for God. Keep doing God's work. He will take care of everything else. When God confronted Elijah after he had run away from Jezebel, he asked him, "What are you doing here, Elijah?" (1 Kings 19:13, NKJV) Then God gave Elijah instructions to anoint three persons. He gave him work to do, indicating that he expected Elijah to carry on with his life and duties during the crisis he faced. It is not what we face in life that matters but how we respond to what we face that truly counts. The iguana which appeared at the top of my water tank disappeared and I haven't seen it since but I continue to see evidence of its existence. If God can take care of an iguana, He most certainly will take care of you.

13

On Policies and Prayer

The reality of evil is evident in every quadrant of the globe. Man is perennially on a desperate search for solutions to personal problems and global challenges. We adopt strategies, enact policies, issue embargos, sign agreements and treaties in the hope of effecting change but, often, to no avail. Why? We must always remember that what we experience in the physical realm is the manifestation of the great controversy between good and evil. A spiritual battle rages. Ephesians 6:12 says, "For we do not wrestle against flesh and blood, but against principalities, against powers, against the rulers of the darkness of this age, against spiritual hosts of wickedness in the heavenly places." The only effective weapon in this warfare is prayer. It is for this reason that we are admonished in 1 Thessalonians 5:17 to "Pray without ceasing." As Christians walking towards the promised land, we have to grasp every opportunity to proclaim that what the world needs is Jesus. What the world needs is prayers. Evil will manifest itself in various forms until Jesus returns when He will "wipe away every tear from their eyes; there shall be no more death, nor sorrow, nor crying. There shall be no more pain, for the former things have passed away." (Revelation 21:4) Prayer, however, can invoke God's mercy and cause policies that create meaningful change to be passed.

Unleashing the Weapon of Prayer

In Queen Esther's time, three days of fasting and prayer reversed a planned genocide (Esther chapters 4-8). The God whom Esther, Mordecai and the rest of the Jews petitioned is the same God that we serve today. He hasn't changed. He cannot change. God Himself declared in Malachi 3:6,"For I am the Lord, I do not change." God's mercies endure forever. No matter what the distressing circumstances are, we have to interpret every problem as an instance of the spiritual battle that rages on. Fasting and Prayer are the weapons of our warfare. The actions of Queen Esther in addressing Haman's threat is instructive in how we should approach the battles we face. We have to formulate strategies to confront evil. Esther's banquet served to make the King receptive to her concerns and it placed Haman in a position to determine his own fate. Moreover, her decision to include the whole nation of the Jews in petitioning God's throne is a clear example of the unity that is needed to effect change in circumstances that involve people groups. More prayer, more power. Esther's story also demonstrates that boldness is a necessary attribute in this warfare. WE have to adopt the kind of attitude depicted in Hebrews 13:6, "So we may boldly say: "The LORD is my helper; I will not fear. What can man do to me?"

Fighting in the Final Days

2 Timothy 3:1- 4 states, "But know this, that in the last days perilous times will come: For men will be lovers of themselves, lovers of money, boasters, proud, blasphemers, disobedient to parents, unthankful, unholy, unloving, unforgiving, slanderers, without self-control, brutal, despisers of good, traitors, headstrong, haughty, lovers of pleasure rather than lovers of God," This passage of scripture paints a gloomy picture of life in the final days of Earth's history. These are the times that we live in. We will only be able to endure by following the direction given in God's word:

> Therefore take up the whole armor of God that you may be able to withstand in the evil day, and having done all, to stand. Stand therefore, having girded your waist with truth, having put on the breastplate of righteousness, and having shod your feet with the preparation of the gospel of peace; above all, taking the shield of faith with which you will be able to quench all the fiery darts of the wicked one. And take the helmet of salvation, and the sword of the Spirit, which is the word of God; (Ephesians 6:13-17)

Policies without a clear perspective on what is behind the troubles of the world have limited value. We must pray for God's guidance and direction, His intervention, His grace, his mercy and He will direct us to create policies that truly matter.

14

Who's leading you?

In every sphere of life we are either leading or being led. Some people may passionately object to the idea that they are being led by someone, but to claim that no one is leading you is to deny the fact that someone or some people make decisions that impact your present state and your future prospects. So, who's leading you?

While we are required as Christians to respect those in authority, we should also bear in mind that leaders are people and not all leaders, even church leaders, have attributes that are worth emulating. The Bible is replete with examples of leaders who turned away from God and led their followers astray. From Israel's first king, Saul, to notorious King Ahab, we are shown clearly that we must evaluate our leaders and choose to honour God and God alone.

Pay attention to the heart

When God instructed Samuel to anoint David king of Israel, Samuel had the experience of meeting all of Jesse's older sons and discovering from God's choice that outward appearance and physical stature do not count with God. God looks at the heart and as his followers we should do the same. No man is perfect but a good leader seeks the perfect will of God and his/her heart is revealed in the words that are spoken spontaneously and the actions that are taken without measured calculation. So, how do you determine what is in your leader's heart? The Bible, our Life Guide, dictates that we use the following principles to evaluate leaders.

1. Listen to what is spoken

The words of leaders reveal their core values and what they think about the people they are leading. Numbers chapter 13 gives a critical account of how leaders reveal the true state of their heart through the words they utter. It also demonstrates how the decisions of leaders can impact the lives of their followers.

The entire account of the Israelites experience at this juncture is an illustration of the importance of trust in God, self-efficacy, motivation, as well as the crucial role of leadership in determining the course of history. All the men who were sent to Canaan were leaders. The bible declares that God specifically instructed Moses to send a ruler from each tribe of Israel and Moses "sent them ... all them men who were heads of the children of Israel" (Numbers 13:3, NKJV). They all held the same position but they fell strikingly into two categories and two critical concepts in leadership divided them - attitude and vision. Both became apparent through their words.

The Israelites were tasked with capturing Canaan from its inhabitants. Though God had already promised it to the children of Israel, he still required them to "spy out the land". (Num. 13:1) Notice that he specifically instructed Moses to send leaders. They all held the same position but they were not united in their attitude and vision. Ten decided the task was impossible - the challenges were too great, the obstacles insurmountable; they did not have even a fig of a chance at success.

Caleb and Joshua, on the other hand, examined the task, created a brilliant vision and were eager to start the execution of their mission. If ever there was an expression of trust in executive management (God), self-confidence and belief in the efficacy of the resources at one's disposal, particularly, human resources, it is the address given by Joshua and Caleb to the people of Israel. What remarkable leadership! In my words, the essence of what they said is:

> We have carefully analysed the situation. It is true that the challenges are many and the obstacles are great, but these would crumble in the face of our determination. We have the unwavering support of management and we are well equipped to achieve our goal. We need not fear, we need not cower. Let us move forward with confidence. Victory will be ours. Victory is ours.

Joshua and Caleb had the attitude of winners. They saw themselves as winners and they saw the people they led as winners too. Sadly, the Israelites were already devastated by the reckless pronouncements made by the ten worthless leaders. "We are not able to go up against the people; for they are stronger than we. ... we were like grasshoppers in our own sight, and so we were in their sight" (Num. 13:31, 33). Talk about a pathetic self-concept! The bible indicates that the whole multitude of Israel gullibly accepted the leaders' perception of themselves and their followers. In spite of what they knew about the God they served and their experience of His matchless power, they failed to sieze the opportunity to exercise faith in Him. The ultimate consequence of the kind of leaders the ten were is that, except for Caleb and Joshua, that generation of Israelites never experienced the realisation of the goal. They never reached their destination. God had pronounced, "they certainly shall not see the land of which I swore to their fathers, nor shall any of those who rejected Me see it" (Num. 14:23 NKJV). In Matthew 12:24 Jesus announced, "For out of the abundance of the heart the mouth speaks". Leaders reveal who they truly are by their words so listen carefully to what they say.

2. Watch what is done

The second principle is to pay close attention to what is done. Abram was a leader who demonstrated that the actions of leaders reveal their character. In Genesis 13, we learn that when the herdsmen of Abram's lifestock strove with the herdsmen of Lot's lifestock, Abram did not ignore the situation. He went to

Lot with a direct proposal His action shows that good leaders seek solutions to problems. Secondly, he did not choose the direction Lot should take, he allowed lot to make a choice. Abram proposed to Lot, "If you take the left, then I will go to the right; or if you go to the right, then I will go to the left" (Genesis 13:9 NKJV), and he kept his word. In the very next chapter of Genesis, there is a record of Abram rescuing Lot from captivity. Good leaders protect their followers and rescue them from trouble.

However, our greatest example of the qualities of a good leader does not come from Joshua, Caleb or Abram. Jesus is the greatest example of what a leader should be like. He lived what he expected of His followers. He taught them patiently, he demonstrated love and compassion and he humbly served them. Jesus fulfilled the task of washing the feet of his disciples in the ultimate demonstration of servant leadership. By His words and actions, He showed that He truly cared for His followers. All leaders should care about the people who follow them. How does your leader measure up? More significantly, what kind of leader are you?

Evaluate yourself

If you are a leader, remember that you influence others and you should be mindful of the example you set. What traits will people exhibit when they emulate you? Proverbs 16:29 warns us that a violent man enticeth his neighbour, and leadeth him into the way that is not good" while Proverbs 28:10 states, "Whoso causeth the righteous to go astray in an evil way, he shall fall himself into his own pit: but the upright shall have good things in possession". These texts speak of influence. The adjective 'violent' could effectively be replaced by any other negative trait and clearly there is certain and sure punishment for those who negatively influence others but a just reward for those who influence others for good. Proverbs 3:33 makes this even more explicit. It states, "The curse of the Lord is in the house of the wicked: but he blesseth the habitation of the just".

15

Time and time again

Perhaps the greatest gift God has given to us apart from the breath of life is time. We should not take it for granted. None of us knows how long we have to live but we do know that one day we will die for James 4:14 instructs us, "whereas you do not know what will happen tomorrow. For what is your life? It is even a vapor that appears for a little time and then vanishes away" (NKJV) Our times are in God's hands and one day our breathing will cease and God will demand from us an account of how we spent our days. Our eternal destiny will be determined, according to Matthew 24, on how we spend the time God blesses us with. So, as we journey on, let's be intentional about how we treat time. Let's heed the advise in Ecclesiastes 9:10, "Whatever your hand finds to do, do *it* with your might; for *there is* no work or device or knowledge or wisdom in the grave where you are going." Here are six principles that should shape our relationship with time.

1. Time was created for us

We were created to function within the context of time. Time, as represented by day and night and ruled by the sun and moon respectively, was created before man and God declared that it was good. The order of creation is not random. If we study what was created on each day it becomes evident that God had a plan that culminated in the creation of a day of rest. God was intentional in his creation of time. We need wisdom to be intentional in our use of time. The Bible says in Psalm 90:12, "So teach us to number our days, That we may gain a heart of wisdom" (NKJV).

2. Each day is a special blessing

Secondly, each day is a gift given to us by God. Although we can enhance our health and lengthen our life by the lifestyle choices we make, it is God who ultimately decides when our souls are required of us. During the week of creation, God declared, "it was good" upon the work that He had done on that day. Likewise, we should use each day doing good things. Moreover, we should utilise the hours of the day meaningfully and be diligent with whatever our hands find to do. whatever we do with each day must be such that we can declare like God did after every day of creation, "it was good". Ephesians 5:15 -16 admonishes us, "See then that you walk circumspectly, not as fools but as wise redeeming the time, because the days are evil."

3. We do better when we prioritise our activities

Since we have limited time, we have to plan carefully and prioritize our activities. Like God, we must do things in an orderly and sequential manner. I am confident that the great God of heaven and earth could have completed all of creation in one day or less. But did he? No, he deliberately had a single focus for each day. If we follow God's example, we would not try to cram 101 things into a day. Do only what is essential for that day. Calmly and efficiently perform what you set out to do each day. Don't rush. I have found that the old adage, "More haste, less speed", is absolutely correct for when we rush, we make mistakes, we skip essential steps, and we knock things over. The corrective actions we have to take utilize more time and set us further back from our goals. Have calm, unrushed, focus driven days.

4. Make progress with time

Make sure what is done in each day takes you closer to your overall goal for your week, your month, your life. It is also important to ensure that what is accomplished at each stage can be supported by what was accomplished earlier. The crowning act of God's creation was man and each day brought Him closer to the ideal circumstances for that ultimate goal to be accomplished and sustained. All that was essential for man's welfare was in place before he was created. Through the process of creation, God established a principle for us to follow when we set out to accomplish great things. We must always ask ourselves whether the circumstances that would make our project sustainable are in place. If we take the time to ascertain that what is accomplished can be sustained, we would save ourselves much frustration later on.

5. Evaluate your accomplishments

Another important use of our time is that spent evaluating what we have accomplished. Moses records that at the end of each day of creation God evaluated what He had accomplished. Repeatedly, we read, "and God saw that it was good". Make it a practice to evaluate your day, your week, and what you have accomplished in your life to date. Evaluating puts things in perspective and motivates us to progress or adopt corrective measures so that we optimize our use of time.

6. Capitalise on God's provision for rest

Finally, we must rest. After six days of creation, God took the seventh day to rest. A whole day to rest tells me that rest is important. In fact, I am confident that the great God of the universe was not physically exhausted after speaking the elements of creation into being and fashioning man from the dust of the ground. He wanted to put a seal on His creation and set us an example so that we could live optimum lives. We must rest, and if we are true to God's example, we would earn the rest by working first. But, make no mistake, God created a day of rest at the end of creation because he wanted rest to be an essential aspect of man's life.

Knowing these six principles will not magically transform your relationship with time but being conscious of them and taking the time to contemplate on each one is an essential step to maximizing your day and using your time to the glory of God. Time is a special gift from the Creator and it is our responsibility to relate to it like it is a gift. Following the principles that are evident from creation week, we can live in harmony with time.

16

Walking in the Dessert

We have all had periods of our lives when things were not going quite as we expected. During these times, it seems like we are walking in the dessert. It might have been a promotion that did not materialise, a pregnancy that was not happening, a partner we were not meeting or we were not being as productive as we would like in our various pursuits. Perhaps, we were productive but what we produced was not getting the attention or acclaim that we expected. One of the challenges of life is accepting that life has seasons. Ecclesiastes 3:1-8 says:

> To everything *there is* a season,
> A time for every purpose under heaven:
> ² A time to be born,
> And a time to die;
> A time to plant,

And a time to pluck *what is* planted;
[3] A time to kill,
And a time to heal;
A time to break down,
And a time to build up;
[4] A time to weep,
And a time to laugh;
A time to mourn,
And a time to dance;
[5] A time to cast away stones,
And a time to gather stones;
A time to embrace,
And a time to refrain from embracing;
[6] A time to gain,
And a time to lose;
A time to keep,
And a time to throw away;
[7] A time to tear,
And a time to sew;
A time to keep silence,
And a time to speak;
[8] A time to love,
And a time to hate;
A time of war,
And a time of peace.

There are periods of joy and periods of sorrow; times when you skip across a savannah and times when you trudge through the dessert. In all of these times, we must remember God's promise to never leave us nor forsake us. The right mindset and attitude will bring you through any situation. It is also important to remember that when, to our finite minds, nothing seems to be happening, God is preparing us for His purpose. Joseph was sold into slavery and was imprisoned on a false accusation. It seemed that his life was fruitless but God was preparing the way for him to save countless lives. (See Genesis 39-47) During the decades that Moses lived among the Midianites, it might have seemed that he was not maximising his potential. After all, he was raised by Pharaoh's daughter and had all the advantages his privileged position rendered. Yet, God was preparing him to be the greatest deliverer of all times. When nothing special seems to be happening for you or those who are walking with God, remember to put your trust in God and depend on Him completely. There are also three key observations that we should bear in mind.

Something is always happening

First of all, every situation is a key part of the process of attaining God's purpose. Have confidence that the clock doesn't stop in God's master plan and if it does, that's part of the plan! During periods of apparent barrenness, something is happening. We might not be aware of the chiseling and polishing that is taking place to fit us for what the future holds, but we should not despair when we do not seem to be getting ahead or doing as much as we would like.

Observe nature. There are so many lessons in nature that demonstrate that apparent inactivity is not wasted time. We all know that something is happening in a seed that lies in the earth before the first cotyledons emerge. What's happening in a chrysalis before a magnificent butterfly emerges? Because we cannot see the process does not make the exceptionally spectacular transformation any less real. You might want to argue that my analogy is faulty and when your plans, hopes and aspirations are not coming to fruition, it's just that, nothing happening, period. This will only be true if you cease to live during that period. Once you are alive, trusting God and holding on to your dreams, something is happening. Maybe, you are developing skills and attitudes that will fit you for the future without even being aware of it. Maybe, you're acquiring knowledge that will become critical when things begin to happen for you. I just know that when nothing seems to be happening, it is often our perspective that is skewed.

Seek guidance from God

Never fail to consider the possibility that you might be moving in the wrong direction. The Bible says in Proverbs 3:6 "In all your ways acknowledge Him, And He shall direct your paths." Surely, God will lead you if you allow Him to lead your life. If you are facing stumbling block after stumbling block and you have sought God's guidance, He might be leading you to explore alternatives. Don't be stubborn. While it is good to hold on to your dreams, a period of dearth, might be an opportunity for you to discover that you have talents that you were not previously aware of. It might also be a chance for you to assess whether what you want is really in your best interest. Maybe it might be in your interest but not in your **best** interest if it will have a negative impact on your relationship with God.

It may also be that God is steering you away from something that will have a negative impact on those you love. If the people you love are unhappy, you would definitely be unhappy too. So, while you are holding on to your dreams, have an open mind. God might have something bigger and better for you which you will discover as you explore alternatives. Remember, "all things work together for good to those who love God, to those who are the called according to his purpose." (Romans 8:28, NKJV). So, when nothing seems to be happening, have faith and be kind to yourself and others.

Attitude lifts or lowers our prospects

Finally, check your attitude. We should not be going around feeling sorry for ourselves and complaining when life is not progressing as we wish. Neither should we complain about, nor condemn others who do not seem to be making as much progress as we expect them to be making at any stage in their life. Be patient with yourself and be patient with those around you. The golden rule is applicable here. Furthermore, we should consider whether our attitude might not be our stumbling block. Be positive. Develop the fruit of the spirit (Gal. 5:22-26). Those who possess the fruit, bear fruits. Some time ago I saw a poster which read, "A bad attitude is like a flat tyre, you won't get anywhere unless you change it". So true. Once you have the confidence that you are being prepared for the future and you have the right attitude, then just be patient. Your time will come and when it does, it just might exceed your greatest expectations. Just wait on the Lord. Isaiah 40:31 says:

> But those who wait on the Lord
> Shall renew their strength;
> They shall mount up with wings like eagles,
> They shall run and not be weary,
> They shall walk and not faint.

17

Who is advising you?

Proverbs 11:14 says, "Where *there is* no counsel, the people fall; But in the multitude of counselors *there is* safety". Giving and taking advice is a communication act that represents an important aspect of how human beings relate to each other. The Oxford Advanced Learners Dictionary defines the word *advice* simply as, "opinion given about what to do or how to behave" The Bible admonishes us to seek counsel or advice but it is important to note that the source and substance of the opinions that we receive matter more than we often realise. Like that which the serpent gave to Eve in the Garden of Eden, advice is sometimes unsolicited and seemingly simple, but the consequences of adhering to it could be destructive. The entire course of human history has turned on the words, "You will not surely die. For God knows that in the day you eat of it your eyes will be opened and you will be like God, knowing good and evil" (Gen.3:4-5, NKJV). Eve should have rejected the advice on two counts: A talking serpent gave it to her and it was in direct contradiction to the authoritative word of her Creator. But the source and substance of the opinion that was given to her were ignored. Eve took the advice of the serpent, man was driven from the garden and human beings die one breath at a time from the moment they are born. As consequential as the piece of advice that the serpent gave to Eve has been, it is not the passage of scripture that I find most instructive on the subject of receiving counsel.

Soliciting advice for important decisions

1Kings 12:1-14 recounts an intriguing story. King Rehoboam was newly crowned and as an inexperienced King he knew that he needed to seek advice before making important decisions. When his subjects, led by Jeroboam came to him and said, "Your father made our yoke heavy; now therefore, lighten the burdensome service of your father; and his heavy yoke which he put on us, and we will serve you" (vs 4), he responded with the words, "Depart for three days, then come back to me." How did Rehoboam spend the three days? Verses 6 to 11 are pivotal to the story. First, the Bible says, "King Rehoboam consulted the elders who stood before his father Solomon while he lived, and he said, 'How do you advise me to answer these people?' And they spoke to him saying, 'if you will be a servant to these people today, and serve them, and answer them, and speak good words to them, then they will be your servants forever.' As a newly appointed, inexperienced leader, Rehoboam did one right thing. He sought advice. Rehoboam sought and received advice on how to act but it's one thing to seek advice and quite another to accept it.

The counsel of the elders – servant leadership

Let's analyse the situation. What the subjects requested represented a radical change in the kind of governance that existed in the kingdom. The people had grown weary of the burdensome, onerous leadership style of King Solomon and wanted a change. This paradigm shift would require a rejection of the system which Rehoboam had inherited and an implementation of a new system of kindness, consideration, participatory decision making and mutual satisfaction. The older, experienced elders with whom he consulted first were closely acquainted with the practices of the system that existed. The advice given to Rehoboam by the elders represents a style of leadership currently lauded as the most effective style of leadership for any cultural context. "If you will be a servant to these people ... they will be your servants forever" seems paradoxical but it represents a profound truth about effective leadership. An effective leader is a servant leader. A servant leader is one who is responsive to the needs of his/her followers. This type of leader is humble, desires to help his/her followers achieve self-actualisation, accepts people for who they are, is kind, honest, dependable and trustworthy. When followers realise that they are valued as individuals, they repond with love, loyalty and faithful service. The elders were advising Rehoboam from the perspective of individuals who had lived and worked under Solomon and knew from experience that Solomon's model of leadership was ineffective. But Rehoboam rejected their advice.

The counsel of peers – limited perspective

Instead of implementing the change which the people requested and the elders recommended, Rehoboam consulted with young men who had grown up with him. I believe this piece of information is provided in the story for a reason. The fact that the young men had grown up with Rehoboam suggests that they were no more equipped than he was to make this important decision. They lacked the necessary perspective and values. Their advice was a complete antithesis to what the elders had proposed. This does not suggest that the counsel of youth is always erroneous or misguided but in this situation, historical knowledge, which the youth lacked, was advantageous. The young men proposed that Rehoboam reject the requests of his people and become what was essentially a dragon king, a ruthless dictator. On the third day, the people returned to Rehoboam to hear his decision. Verse 13 states, "Then the king answered the people roughly, and rejected the advice which the elders had given him; and he spoke to them according to the advice of the young men, saying 'My father made your yoke heavy but I will add to your yoke; my father chastised you with whips but I will chastise you with scourges!" Thus, Rehoboam sought advice from two sources and made a choice which shaped the course of his reign and determined his ignominious legacy.

Advice and factors of merit

One crucial lesson to be learnt from this story is that all advice do not have the same merit. When we receive counsel, we should have criteria for evaluating the value of the advice we receive. The fact is that whether you seek advice or not, people will take it upon themselves to advise you. Those who are newly married, newly appointed to a management position, new mothers or new to any role can expect that advice will factor in their communication with others. Sift every piece of advice you receive. Pay attention to the source and substance of the opinions that guide your decision making. What values and principles do the people who advise you represent? I know it could be difficult to decide whose opinion to accept and what decision to make in certain circumstances but we are not left without a rubric. The infallible word of God is our guide. We should never fail to use it. Decisions regarding your relationship with others should always be fruit-flavoured. Yes, take advice that represent the fruit of the spirit. Galatians 5:22 says, "But the fruit of the spirit is love, joy, peace, longsuffering, kindness, goodness, faithfulness, gentleness, self control". Moreover, Micah 6:8 says, "He has shown you, O man, what is good; And what does the Lord require of you But to do justly, To love mercy, And to walk humbly with your God?" That's your criteria for determining what advice to take.

18

Hope lingers still . . .

Just before Jesus departed from earth, He uttered some very comforting words to his followers. Those words provide hope for those of us who are walking with Him. He said, "Let not your heart be troubled; you believe in God, believe also in Me. In My Father's house are many mansions; if it were not so, I would have told you. I go to prepare a place for you. And if I go and prepare a place for you, I will come again and receive you to Myself; that where I am, there you may be also." (John 14:1-3 NKJV) This promise should strengthen our resolve to walk with Jesus every day. The road may be rough, slippery, steep or too narrow at times but it leads to a beautiful place. Stay on course; you started with the hope of eternal life and that hope lingers still.

Contrasting circumstances; symbols of hope

Have you ever seen a tree that was equally alive and dead? Some years ago I was out on my morning exercise when my eyes were drawn to a peculiar sight. A few yards off the road I was walking on, in a forested area, was a tree that was half alive and apparently half dead. I stood and stared at it for several minutes. The fully grown tree had luxuriant green leaves on one half; the other half had dry, brittle branches. On the half that was alive and sprouting green leaves, there was absolutely no sign of decay. In contrast, the other half appeared hopelessly dead. To my finite mind, no amount of sunshine and rain could reverse its condition. Immediately, I thought that the unidentified tree was a symbol for many facets of life. In this world, where so much seems to be dying, there is still much that is worthy of admiration. There is a lot to fear but amidst the things that engender fear, there is hope.

Belief in God's promises brings hope

Hope changes our perspective. Right now you may be grappling with issues which seem hopeless but it does not matter how grave your present situation is, God, with whom all things are possible, can breathe life into it. Your health can be restored, your family can be strengthened, you can flourish financially and your dying spirituality can be rejuvenated if you embrace the eternal promises in God's word.

The Bible declares in Romans 6:23, *"For the wages of sin is death, but the gift of God is eternal life in Christ Jesus our*

Lord." (NKJV) We have all sinned, but none of us needs to die. There is hope of eternal life in Christ Jesus. We have accepted the gift of eternal life so it is our responsibility to share this good news with others and help them to make the right choice. Many are despairing but those of us who are walking with God can help our fellowmen to understand that God has made the provision for the whole world to enjoy peace in this present life and eternal joy in the new Earth.

Hope in the cross

The cross is a symbol of hope that one day all the trouble on the Earth will cease. It is a symbol of hope that every dire situation we face can change, or God can give us grace to endure to the end. The Saviour's death and resurrection should give us the assurance that we can trust the word of God and all the promises that He lovingly made to us. Certainly, we could be reassured that we can cast all our cares upon Him for he cares for us. The hope that we have as Christians should be extended to the world. The story of Jesus' death and resurrection should be shared, not just during the season when the world is celebrating Easter, but at every opportunity that is presented to us.

Hope in the second coming of Jesus

The world needs to know that one day, Jesus Christ, who did not just die but rose again, will return in majestic splendour and all things will be made new. There will be no health challenges, absolutely no pandemics, and no broken families. Definitely, we will not lose our loved ones to the sting of death. There will be no famine, no wars, and no more fear. Just joy forevermore. Revelation 21:1-4 says:

> *Now I saw a new heaven and a new earth, for the first heaven and the first earth had passed away. Also there was no more sea. Then I, John, saw the holy city, New Jerusalem, coming down out of heaven from God, prepared as a bride adorned for her husband. And I heard a loud voice from heaven saying, "Behold, the tabernacle of God is with men, and He will dwell with them, and they shall be His people. God Himself will be with them and be their God. And God will wipe away every tear from their eyes; there shall be no more death, nor sorrow, nor crying. There shall be no more pain, for the former things have passed away.*

Isn't that worth hoping and living for? It certainly is, so find peace in spite of what's happening around you. Trust that all of it is subject to the perfect will of God.

About the Author

Desryn Tessa Ann Collins is a woman of God. Her experiences as a wife, mother, sister, sister-friend, neighbour, immigrant, lifelong Educator and passionate Christian have provided her with a unique depth of understanding of the many issues that confront us in life. She resides in St John's, Antigua which has been her adopted country since  1995 when she migrated from Guyana, South America. For nearly thirty years, she has been married to Albert Michael Collins and they have three adult sons - Rhodri, Aldryn and Vaughn who keep her grounded. She lives by the conviction that God loves us with an everlasting love so we can rest peacefully in all of our experiences.

Printed in the United States
by Baker & Taylor Publisher Services

Printed in the United States
by Baker & Taylor Publisher Services